Stars Inside Her
journaling with bone sighs...

ISBN: 978-0-9815440-7-6
bone sigh books
www.BoneSighBooks.com
www.BoneSighArts.com

Please don't steal any of this work,
if you want to use something, just ask.

Cover art by Noah Urban
www.BFGproductions.com

Thank you, Shari, for the inspiration!

Stars Inside Her
journaling with bone sighs...

by you & me (terri st. cloud)

✦✦✦✦✦

I have wanted to create a bone sigh journal for years. Picturing large, hard-cover books with brilliant, colorful watercolors mixed all through out, I would get swept away with the possibilities. When I came back down to earth and tried to put my rarin'-to-go toes into the practical waters of making it happen, things like keeping it sweatshop free, and keeping the prices low for people to actually be able to buy a copy made those very toes curl back in disappointment.

It's been an idea that's been hanging out on the back burner for years. Until a customer called one day. She told me that she was taking the bone sighs one at a time and journaling with them! Oh my gosh! Now, I had thought of mixing bone sighs around on blank pages, mixing them here and there to decorate. But to actually use them to guide the journaling...well, that's an idea I had never thought of!

I gasped with delight and jotted a note down so I wouldn't forget. Well, I didn't really need that note. I was too excited with the idea to forget. And the beauty of it all was that at the same time the idea hit, an understanding also landed in.

Our very first book, 'honor yourself' was created in honor of someone I lost. A young woman who couldn't find her way out of the darkness. The design for that book was developed with that young woman in mind. We wanted something she would have been able to afford without having to worry about it, something she would have been able to slip in a purse or glove compartment or locker. Something that didn't overwhelm, but touched. Something that would remind her that she mattered and counted.

All our books since then have followed that design. And what landed into my head was that right after 'honor yourself,' this journal would be the next most important book to have in that very same design. If we could offer the same thing for someone in a journal form, with the bone sighs guiding them just a tiny bit, well, how cool would that be? And what an honor!

I get so caught up in this world of mine, I forget that not everyone knows what a bone sigh is! 'Bone sighs' are the quotes that I write, these things that are a mix of poetry, thoughts, meanderings and stories. I used to be picky and say that a bone sigh was one of those quotes mixed with the art that I created. Well, it can be that too...but doesn't have to be. I've come to realize that a bone sigh is something that touches you deeply and comes from your depths. We all have them. Every single one of us. A bone sigh comes in many, many forms!

For this book though, a bone sigh is the quote you'll find at the top of every other page. At least, that's where they start. You'll be adding your own bone sighs all through out as you write what's inside of you.

The idea is to give you a starting point to dive into your own thoughts. Something that spurs you on and gets that pen moving. No one needs to be a 'writer' to write. All you need is a pen or pencil and a willingness to look inside. And you know what I'm thinking? I'm thinking that we all have stars inside us! I really think so! A lot of us have forgotten them or covered them, but they're there. And I'm thinking that we all have so much beauty and light to find. It's all at our fingertips. If this journal can in any way help you do that, then I truly am grateful. What a treat to be able to journey with you! Here's to the stars inside all of us!

and she honored the holiness inside her...

more than anything –
i want to trust a journey that i don't understand.

maybe the holding stunts you, she thought.
maybe growth is release, non gripping, flowing,
ever forward, ever motion, ever new.

maybe being brave is no more than staring down
the 'less than' feeling and stepping up to
the 'i am worthy' feeling.

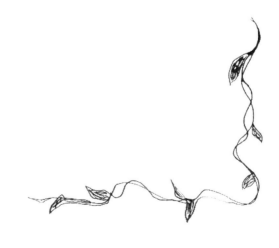

it's not about controlling.
it's about being present, being open. being aware.
and allowing it to come.

she'd been fighting herself so long now,
the idea of trusting herself seemed foreign.
and yet...if she could trust...if she could just trust herself
~she just might discover the best friend she's ever known.

— ♡ . ♡ . ♡ . ♡ . ♡ . ♡ . ♡ . ♡ . ♡ . ♡ —

don't follow the blue people, she said.
they dull you and numb you...travel down to your cave.
there you will discover your depths and your heights.
and it is there you gather the explosives to
light your life on fire.

some believed in her.

others did not.

she joined the circle of believers and rejoiced with them.

it is your truth. your power. your soul.
guard it with all you have.
don't let anyone's misconceptions steal it.
including your own.

maybe...just maybe...
all you can do is love with all you have inside of you.
and maybe that love will heal your wounds.

scratch the surface of her joy and you will find a well of sorrow. dive into the well and discover her spring of hope. follow that spring to the river of her strength, compassion and faith...immerse yourself in her river and you will have touched her soul.

she wanted to honor the wise one inside herself
but didn't know how.
the answer echoed from her depths ~ see who you are.
become more of who you are. delight in your soul.

your inner voice is the voice of the soul...follow it.

it is not enough to find your passion...
you must dive straight into the fire of your fear~
where you can grab it and hold it
until it transforms you.

she let go of the shame and the guilt. seeing that she couldn't have become who she was without those past mistakes. it was time to honor them and thank them, and know that they were some of the best parts of her.

maybe grace is figuring out it's not all about you.
that people are doing what they're doing for
their own reasons. not yours.
and maybe grace is accepting that.

and she valued herself.

in and out, up and down, over and over she wove her strands of life together. patching hole after hole, eventually she saw it was more than the threads that gave her strength, it was in the very act of weaving itself, that she became strong.

shovel full after shovel full, she unearthed her Self.
kneeling at the beauty that had been buried,
she cleansed it with her tears and lifted her Self
into the Light.

maybe when you really love yourself
you can see beyond that self -
and then maybe you never give yourself away.
maybe you just give.

her eyes opened to her own beauty and the ground shook.

you can try to feed the bear but he will never get enough.
the best thing to do is feed yourself.

grab your spirit. grab your heart...hold it, hold it close,
hold it up high...let it shine, believe in it, love it,
nurture it, share it, grow it, and never ever give it up,
label it or change it to make someone else happy.

it is in the commitment to trust that mountains begin to move. it is in the commitment to love that walls begin to crumble, and it is in the commitment to one's self that worlds unimagined begin to become real.

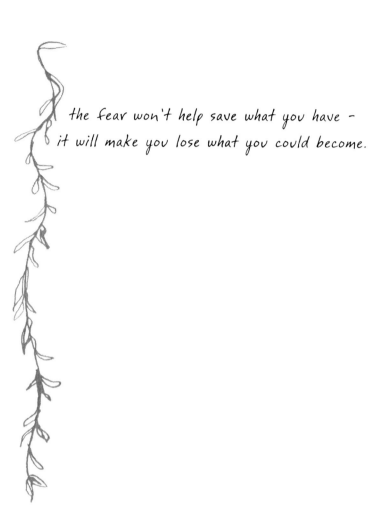

the fear won't help save what you have –
it will make you lose what you could become.

she called upon the different parts of herself for help.
if she was going to make it, she needed to accept them all,
unite them all, and believe in them all.
it was time for a huddle of tremendous proportions.
it was the making of her giant.

it was when she first dared to see her truth, that the
winds howled. after a time, it strengthened her and she
spoke her truth and the earth shook. and when finally, she
believed her truth —the stars rejoiced, the universe opened,
and even her bones sang her song: "I Matter!"

she was scared again. seems she was scared a lot these days.
time for a deep breath and another plunge in.
it was the only way to get to where she wanted to go.
so, in she went.

—honor yourself—honor yourself - honor yourself—

she wasn't them. she couldn't be.
was she going to claim herself as herself
or forever be half-way between worlds?

if i could teach you anything -
it would be to hear your heart,
and to know your beauty,
and to believe in your possibilities

she could never go back and make some of the details pretty. all she could do was move forward and make the whole beautiful.

i will not allow myself to be less than i am
to meet anybody's expectations.

why do you look for it over there? the voice asked.
it's all inside you. look within. embrace what you see.
and dance with all that is you.

at times she called it baggage, dragging its heavy weight along. other times she called it fuel, using it to push her forward. now she called it history in her veins and just accepted it as part of her life flow.

you, my child, are not throw away material.
you are made up of the fabric of the universe -
threaded with the very dust of the stars.
know it. accept it. and allow it to shine forth.

strength lies in the opening of the heart -

from her sorrow she found compassion.
from her grief she learned understanding.
and from her journey she became real.

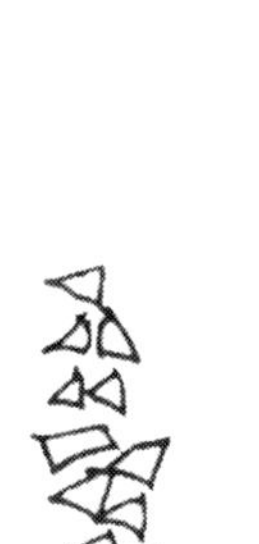

perhaps power is letting go of the grip of the past
and standing empty handed facing the future.

it is in your solo flight that your wings become filled with power, the clouds part, and the heavens open.

it was her heart she needed to open - not the door.
the door was wide open - all she needed to do was dare.

they were wrong.
she was okay just the way she was.

there were pieces of her heart lying around cold and lonely.
unhonored.
gradually she gathered them together.
taking her heart back, she made it hers again.

she took her power back ~
without permission.

melting,
i lose the me,
and begin to touch the all.

she not only had a gift to offer the world,
she had a gift to offer herself.
maybe it didn't matter so much if the world
held it. maybe what mattered was that she did.

it wasn't about taking power away from them.
it was about giving power to herself.
and then they didn't matter anymore.
she moved on. and it all just was.

'there's something inside of you, she said. a flame. a gorgeous flame of light. every action you take affects the flame. some actions make it shine brighter. some make it flicker and dim. and some grow it and make it bigger inside. every moment counts to this flame. every action matters.' she held her face to the girl's and whispered, 'dance with honesty and trust thru your journey, and you will grow your flame. grow your flame , and you will ignite the world.'

to have joy you must make it. and take it. saying you want it isn't enough. maybe that's with everything...saying you want it isn't enough. make it. take it.

know it is yours.

she reached as deep as she could inside her pain.
somewhere in there was a piece of
herself she needed to forgive.
and only then could her healing be complete.

the mud puddle was back there.
exactly where she had left it. it wouldn't move.
for that was the nature of mud puddles.
but she would, for that was the nature of her.

i can never go back.
only forward.
ever deeper.

and the fist became the open hand. she refused to beat herself any longer. speaking words of kindness, she gently touched her hair, looked into her own eyes and took the first step towards love.

maybe offering something to the world is living
what you would want to offer.
maybe it's not any more than living it.
and maybe that's the hardest thing of all...

Breinigsville, PA USA
28 October 2010
248198BV00001B/2/P